CAUSES AND PERMANENT SOLUTION TO AUTISM

Knowing The Causes And Permanent Treatment Solution To Autism Individual To Live A Healthy Life

Dr. Mike Fredrick

TABLE OF CONTENTS

INTRODUCTION

Autism Spectrum Disorder (ASD) is a developmental condition that affects how individuals perceive and interact with the world around them. It is characterized by challenges in social communication, repetitive behaviors, and restricted interests. Autism is described as a "spectrum" because it manifests differently in every individual, ranging from mild to more profound challenges. While some individuals with autism may excel in specific areas, others may require significant support in daily activities.

ASD is not a singular condition but rather a complex interplay of neurological, genetic, and environmental factors. Its prevalence has been increasing over the years, partly due to improved awareness and diagnostic practices. This has sparked global discussions about understanding autism, providing adequate support, and fostering inclusivity.

Importance of a Comprehensive Approach

Understanding the causes of autism and identifying effective interventions require a multi-faceted approach. The uniqueness of each individual's experience with autism highlights the importance of tailored support strategies. Efforts to address autism must shift from seeking a "cure" to promoting acceptance, inclusion, and support for neurodiverse individuals.

This document explores the potential causes of autism, the concept of a "permanent solution," and practical strategies for enhancing the lives of those with ASD and their families. By delving into research and advocacy, we aim to promote a deeper understanding of autism and emphasize the value of embracing neurodiversity.

CHAPTER 1
Causes of Autism

Autism Spectrum Disorder (ASD) arises from a complex interaction of genetic, environmental, and neurological factors. Although the precise causes remain unknown, significant progress has been made in identifying contributing influences. Below is an exploration of these factors:

Genetic Factors

Genetics play a significant role in autism. Studies indicate that autism often runs in families, and specific genes are associated with increased susceptibility to the condition.

Gene Mutations: Variations in multiple genes, such as those involved in brain development and synaptic communication, have been linked to autism.
Hereditary Influence: If a family member has autism, the likelihood of another individual in the family being diagnosed increases.

Genetic Syndromes: Certain genetic conditions, such as Fragile X syndrome, Rett syndrome, and tuberous sclerosis, are associated with autism-like traits.

Prenatal and Perinatal Factors

Events during pregnancy and around birth may contribute to autism:

Advanced Parental Age: Older parental age at the time of conception has been associated with a higher risk of autism.
Maternal Health: Certain maternal infections, diabetes, or complications during pregnancy can increase the likelihood of autism.
Birth Factors: Premature birth, low birth weight, or lack of oxygen during delivery (hypoxia) may impact brain development, contributing to autism.

Environmental Influences
Environmental factors, particularly during critical developmental periods, can interact with genetic predispositions:

Exposure to Toxins: Prenatal exposure to certain chemicals, such as pesticides or heavy metals, has been linked to a higher risk of autism.
Medications During Pregnancy: Use of certain medications during pregnancy (e.g., valproic acid or thalidomide) has been associated with autism.
Nutritional Factors: Deficiencies in essential nutrients (e.g., folic acid) during pregnancy may increase susceptibility.

Neurological Factors
Differences in brain structure and function are often observed in individuals with autism:

Brain Connectivity: Atypical connections between different brain regions may contribute to the unique sensory, cognitive, and behavioral characteristics of autism.

Neurotransmitter Imbalances: Abnormal levels of neurotransmitters such as serotonin and dopamine have been implicated in autism.

Early Brain Development: Differences in the growth and organization of neurons during early life stages may underlie autistic traits.

The causes of autism are multifactorial, with genetic predispositions interacting with environmental and neurological factors. While research continues to uncover the complex mechanisms behind autism, it is essential to focus on understanding and supporting individuals with ASD, rather than pathologizing their experiences.

CHAPTER 2
Challenges and Impact of Autism

Autism Spectrum Disorder (ASD) affects individuals differently, resulting in a wide range of challenges and impacts on daily life. These can vary depending on the severity of symptoms, the presence of co-occurring conditions, and the level of support provided. Below is an exploration of the key challenges faced by individuals with autism and their broader impact on families, communities, and society.

Social Communication Challenges

One of the hallmark characteristics of autism is difficulty in social communication and interaction.

Understanding Social Cues: Individuals may struggle to interpret facial expressions, tone of voice, or body language.

Language and Speech: Some individuals experience delayed speech development or may be nonverbal, requiring alternative communication methods.

Building Relationships: Forming and maintaining friendships or other relationships can be challenging due to differences in social behavior or communication style.

Behavioral Patterns

Autistic individuals often exhibit repetitive behaviors and restricted interests that can impact their daily lives.

Repetitive Behaviors: Examples include hand-flapping, rocking, or repeating certain phrases. These behaviors can be self-soothing but may seem unusual to others.
Rigid Routines: A strong preference for routine and predictability may lead to distress when unexpected changes occur.
Special Interests: Deep focus on specific topics or activities can be a source of joy but may limit engagement with broader experiences.

Sensory Processing Differences
Sensory sensitivities are common in autism, often affecting how individuals experience and respond to their environment.

Hypersensitivity: Over-responsiveness to sensory input, such as loud noises, bright lights, or certain textures, can lead to discomfort or meltdowns.
Hyposensitivity: Under-responsiveness to stimuli may result in seeking sensory input through activities like spinning or touching objects repeatedly.
Impact on Daily Life: Sensory challenges can affect participation in school, work, and social settings.

Co-occurring Conditions

Many individuals with autism experience additional medical or psychological conditions, which can compound their challenges.

Anxiety and Depression: High rates of mental health issues are observed, often due to difficulties navigating social environments.
Attention-Deficit/Hyperactivity Disorder (ADHD): Frequently co-occurs with autism, affecting focus and behavior.
Sleep Disorders: Sleep disturbances can exacerbate daytime challenges for individuals and their families.

Broader Impacts
The challenges of autism extend beyond the individual to affect families, communities, and societal systems.

Family Stress: Caregivers may face emotional, financial, and logistical strain in supporting their loved one.
Educational and Workplace Barriers: Many individuals encounter difficulties accessing inclusive education or employment opportunities.
Stigma and Misunderstanding: Misconceptions about autism can lead to social exclusion or discrimination, underscoring the need for greater awareness and acceptance.

The challenges associated with autism are diverse and multifaceted, encompassing social, behavioral, sensory, and co-occurring difficulties. However, with proper support, understanding, and accommodations, individuals with autism can overcome barriers and thrive in their own unique ways. Society benefits greatly from recognizing and celebrating the contributions of neurodiverse individuals while addressing the obstacles they face.

CHAPTER 3
Approaches to Addressing Autism

Given the diversity of experiences within the autism spectrum, there are various approaches to supporting individuals with Autism Spectrum Disorder (ASD). These strategies aim to enhance communication, behavior, social skills, and overall quality of life. The key to effective support lies in early intervention, individualized plans, and continuous support throughout the lifespan. Below are some of the most widely recognized and effective approaches:

Early Intervention Programs

Early intervention is crucial in addressing the developmental needs of children with autism. The earlier the intervention, the better the chances of improving communication, social skills, and adaptive behavior.

Applied Behavior Analysis (ABA): ABA is one of the most widely used therapies for autism, focusing on reinforcing desired behaviors and reducing undesired ones. ABA involves intensive, one-on-one therapy that is structured and data-driven.

Early Start Denver Model (ESDM): This is an early intervention program designed for young children (ages 12-48 months) that combines principles from

ABA with developmental and relationship-based approaches.

Speech Therapy: Speech-language therapy helps individuals develop communication skills, whether verbal or non-verbal, and improves their ability to express needs and understand others.

Occupational Therapy: Occupational therapists assist individuals in developing skills necessary for daily life, such as dressing, eating, and using tools. They also help manage sensory processing issues.

Educational and Behavioral Therapies
Educational approaches and behavioral therapies can significantly improve the functioning of individuals with autism in home, school, and community settings.

Individualized Education Plans (IEPs): In many countries, children with autism are entitled to an IEP, which is a personalized educational plan designed to address specific learning needs. These plans are developed in collaboration with educators, therapists, and parents.

TEACCH (Treatment and Education of Autistic and Communication Handicapped Children): This program emphasizes structured teaching, with a focus on visual supports, routines, and clear instructions. TEACCH helps individuals with autism gain independence by making the environment predictable and structured.

Social Skills Training: Social skills interventions teach children with autism how to interact appropriately in social situations, such as making eye contact, understanding social cues, and engaging in conversations.

Cognitive Behavioral Therapy (CBT): For adolescents and adults with autism, CBT can help address anxiety, depression, and behavioral challenges by teaching coping strategies and problem-solving techniques.

Medical and Technological Support
In addition to therapy and education, some individuals benefit from medical interventions and technology that help manage symptoms or enhance functioning.

Medications: While there is no medication to cure autism, certain medications can help manage symptoms such as anxiety, irritability, or hyperactivity. Commonly prescribed medications include selective serotonin reuptake inhibitors (SSRIs) for anxiety or antipsychotics for severe irritability.

Sensory Integration Therapy: This type of therapy helps individuals with sensory processing difficulties by using various activities that target specific senses, such as touch, hearing, and balance.

Assistive Technology: Devices such as speech-generating devices, communication apps, and specialized software can help non-verbal individuals communicate. Technology also helps with organization, scheduling, and learning.

Neurofeedback: Neurofeedback is an emerging therapy that trains individuals to control brainwave activity, which may improve attention and emotional regulation in some individuals with autism.

Family and Community Support
Family and community play an essential role in the success of interventions and the overall well-being of individuals with autism.

Parent Training and Support: Teaching parents how to manage behavioral challenges, communicate effectively, and implement strategies at home is critical. Support groups and counseling can also help families cope with stress.

Community Inclusion: Creating inclusive communities involves making social and recreational activities accessible to individuals with autism. This can include programs at schools, workplaces, and public spaces designed to be autism-friendly.

Respite Care: For families, respite care provides temporary relief from caregiving responsibilities, allowing caregivers to rest and recharge. This can help prevent burnout and maintain family dynamics.

Approaches to addressing autism must be individualized and flexible, taking into account each person's unique strengths, challenges, and needs. The combination of early intervention, educational and behavioral therapies, medical support, and community involvement can greatly enhance the lives of individuals with autism and their families. By focusing on each person's potential and providing the right support, individuals with autism can lead fulfilling, productive lives.

CHAPTER 4
The Concept of a Permanent Solution

Autism Spectrum Disorder (ASD) is a neurodevelopmental condition that is lifelong, meaning there is no permanent cure or solution in the traditional sense. However, there is ongoing debate and exploration in the scientific and medical communities about what it means to "address" or "treat" autism, and how society can provide better outcomes for individuals with ASD. The concept of a "permanent solution" for autism requires a nuanced understanding, as autism is not considered a disease that needs to be "cured," but rather a difference in neurodevelopmental functioning.

Why Autism is Not a Disease to Cure

Autism is often framed as a developmental condition rather than a disease. Unlike conditions such as infections or cancers that have defined treatments or cures, autism represents a different way of processing and interacting with the world. Individuals with autism may have unique strengths, such as enhanced memory, attention to detail, or creativity.

The idea of seeking a "permanent solution" to autism can be problematic for several reasons:

Neurodiversity Movement: This movement promotes the understanding that autism is a natural variation of human diversity. Just as people have different abilities, interests, and temperaments, neurodiversity celebrates the fact that there are different ways the brain can function. The goal is not to "fix" autism, but to support individuals in ways that allow them to thrive.

Focus on Acceptance Over Cure: Instead of focusing on curing or eliminating autism, the emphasis is now placed on improving quality of life, increasing societal acceptance, and providing individuals with autism the support they need to succeed in various areas of life.

Understanding the Spectrum: Autism exists on a spectrum, meaning its manifestations vary widely across individuals. Some individuals may require significant support, while others lead independent, successful lives. It's important to recognize these varying needs and focus on personalized solutions rather than a one-size-fits-all cure.

Supporting Neurodiversity
Rather than focusing on finding a permanent cure for autism, the concept of "supporting neurodiversity" emphasizes acceptance, accommodations, and celebration of different ways of thinking and processing. Support for neurodiverse individuals focuses on enhancing their lives without seeking to change the fundamental nature of autism.

Educational Support: Tailored educational programs designed to meet the specific needs of individuals with autism are essential for academic success and social growth. Providing structure, routine, and alternative methods of communication can help students on the spectrum succeed in a traditional school environment.

Social Inclusion: Creating inclusive spaces and opportunities for people with autism to engage in social and community activities fosters belonging and decreases stigma. Peer education and raising awareness about autism can also help bridge the gap in understanding and empathy.

Self-Advocacy and Autonomy: Encouraging individuals with autism to be involved in decisions about their lives, including therapies, career paths, and living arrangements, supports self-determination and independence.

Employment and Vocational Support: Many individuals with autism excel in specific fields, such as technology, art, or research. Providing access to vocational training, job coaching, and inclusive workplaces enables individuals to contribute meaningfully to society.

The idea of a "permanent solution" to autism needs to be reframed. Instead of a cure, the focus should be on creating an inclusive society that embraces neurodiversity and provides the necessary support systems for individuals with autism. By emphasizing acceptance, personalized interventions, and community integration, we can improve the lives of individuals with autism without attempting to change who they are fundamentally. This approach allows individuals with autism to lead fulfilling lives that highlight their unique contributions, strengths, and perspectives.

CHAPTER 5

Strategies for Improving Quality of Life

Improving the quality of life for individuals with Autism Spectrum Disorder (ASD) requires a holistic approach that addresses not only the developmental and behavioral aspects but also emotional, social, and environmental factors. By focusing on tailored interventions, promoting inclusivity, and supporting the individual's well-being, it is possible to help individuals with autism lead fulfilling and meaningful lives. Below are key strategies for improving quality of life for individuals with autism:

Individualized Support Plans

Creating a personalized support plan is crucial for addressing the unique needs of each individual with autism. These plans should focus on the person's strengths, challenges, preferences, and goals.

Assessment and Goal Setting: Regular assessments by professionals (e.g., psychologists, speech therapists, occupational therapists) help identify areas for improvement and guide the development of a customized plan.

Therapeutic Interventions: Depending on the individual's needs, interventions might include Applied Behavior Analysis (ABA), speech therapy, occupational therapy, and social skills training.

Tailoring these therapies to the person's abilities and challenges ensures they are effective.

Skill Development: Focusing on life skills such as self-care, communication, and social skills enhances independence and can boost confidence and self-esteem.

Behavioral Supports: Behavior management plans can help individuals learn to navigate difficult situations and reduce behaviors that may interfere with their daily life (e.g., meltdowns or self-harm).

Family and Caregiver Involvement
Families and caregivers play a central role in supporting individuals with autism. By educating and empowering them, families can provide a more supportive home environment, which enhances the individual's quality of life.

Parent Training: Equipping parents with knowledge of autism, behavioral management techniques, and communication strategies can make a significant difference in how effectively they can support their child.

Respite Care: Caregiving can be demanding. Respite services provide short-term care, allowing caregivers to rest and recharge, which ultimately benefits the entire family dynamic.

Emotional Support for Families: Connecting families with support groups, counseling, or advocacy organizations helps them navigate challenges and avoid burnout.

Community Inclusion
Promoting community inclusion ensures that individuals with autism have opportunities to engage in social activities, develop relationships, and participate fully in society.

Inclusive Education: Creating inclusive educational settings that provide accommodations and support helps children with autism learn alongside their peers. Modifying the curriculum to meet the student's needs while fostering social integration is essential.

Social Opportunities: Providing opportunities for social interaction in community settings (e.g., parks, clubs, after-school activities) encourages individuals with autism to practice social skills and build friendships.

Peer Education: Educating peers about autism and fostering understanding helps reduce stigma, making it easier for individuals with autism to participate in social and recreational activities.
Public Awareness Campaigns: Promoting awareness and understanding about autism can lead to more inclusive and accessible public spaces,

reducing barriers and creating a more welcoming environment.

Employment and Vocational Training
For adults with autism, meaningful employment is an important factor in enhancing quality of life. Employment not only provides financial independence but also fosters a sense of purpose and belonging.

Vocational Training: Programs that teach job-specific skills and provide workplace readiness training help individuals with autism prepare for the workforce.

Job Placement Services: Specialized job coaches and placement services can assist individuals in finding suitable employment opportunities that align with their strengths and interests.
Workplace Accommodations: Employers can make reasonable accommodations (e.g., adjusting work hours, providing sensory-friendly environments) to help individuals with autism succeed in the workplace.

Supporting Career Development: Ongoing support in the form of mentoring, skill-building, and professional development can help individuals with autism grow in their careers and become more independent.

Emotional and Mental Health Support
Many individuals with autism experience co-occurring conditions like anxiety, depression, or stress. Addressing mental health is crucial to improving overall well-being and quality of life.

Cognitive Behavioral Therapy (CBT): CBT can help individuals with autism address anxiety, depression, and other emotional challenges. By learning coping strategies and reframing negative thought patterns, individuals can improve their emotional regulation.

Mindfulness and Relaxation Techniques: Incorporating mindfulness, relaxation exercises, and sensory breaks into daily routines can help reduce stress and increase emotional resilience.

Psychological Counseling: For individuals with autism, having access to counseling services (for individuals or families) can provide emotional support and strategies for coping with challenges.

Assistive Technology and Tools
Technology can play a vital role in enhancing communication, learning, and daily functioning for individuals with autism.

Communication Devices: For non-verbal individuals, speech-generating devices or communication apps (such as Proloquo2Go) enable them to express their needs and thoughts.

Learning Apps: Specialized apps designed to help individuals with autism practice language, math, social skills, and more can be a powerful tool for learning and development.

Sensory Tools: Sensory-friendly technology, such as noise-canceling headphones or weighted blankets, can help individuals manage sensory sensitivities and create a calm environment.

Improving the quality of life for individuals with autism requires a combination of individualized support, community inclusion, family involvement, and specialized interventions. By focusing on the person's strengths, needs, and preferences, and by promoting acceptance and understanding in society, we can ensure that individuals with autism lead fulfilling lives. With the right strategies and resources, individuals on the autism spectrum can thrive, reach their potential, and actively contribute to their families and communities.

CHAPTER 6
Research and Advocacy

Research and advocacy are essential pillars in advancing the understanding of Autism Spectrum Disorder (ASD) and improving the lives of individuals with autism. Through research, we gain insights into the causes, treatments, and effective support systems for autism, while advocacy promotes acceptance, inclusion, and the rights of individuals with autism. Together, these efforts help create a more supportive and inclusive world for neurodiverse individuals.

Current Advances in Autism Research

Research on autism is continually evolving, with new findings contributing to a deeper understanding of the condition and its management. Key areas of current research include:

Genetic Research: Scientists are exploring the genetic underpinnings of autism to identify specific genes and mutations linked to ASD. This could lead to improved early diagnosis and better-targeted interventions. Understanding the genetic components of autism can also shed light on how environmental factors interact with genetic predispositions.

Neuroimaging and Brain Research: Advances in brain imaging techniques, such as functional magnetic resonance imaging (fMRI), are providing more information about how the brains of individuals with autism function differently. This research could help identify biomarkers for autism, leading to earlier and more accurate diagnoses, as well as more personalized treatments.

Early Diagnosis and Intervention: Researchers are focused on developing more effective tools for early diagnosis, as earlier intervention has been shown to lead to better long-term outcomes. Studies are also investigating the best types of therapies and interventions during early childhood to improve social, cognitive, and communication skills.

Therapeutic Advances: There is ongoing research into new therapies for autism, including pharmacological treatments, behavioral therapies, and innovative approaches like neurofeedback. Studies are exploring how these therapies might work in combination and their long-term effects on individuals with autism.

Autism Across the Lifespan: Most research has traditionally focused on children, but there is an increasing focus on adults with autism. This includes studies on the challenges faced by adults in education, employment, and independent living, as well as the mental health needs of autistic adults.

Role of Advocacy in Promoting Inclusivity
Advocacy plays a crucial role in ensuring that individuals with autism have the same opportunities and rights as anyone else. Advocates work to increase awareness, reduce stigma, and promote policies that support individuals with autism. Key advocacy efforts include:

Raising Awareness: Autism advocacy organizations and campaigns help educate the public about the spectrum of autism, its characteristics, and how it affects individuals. Awareness campaigns aim to reduce misconceptions, stigma, and discrimination. Public awareness also helps build support for policies and practices that accommodate and include individuals with autism in all aspects of society.

Legislative Advocacy: Advocates work with policymakers to create and pass laws that protect the rights of individuals with autism. This includes advocating for educational accommodations (such as Individualized Education Plans or IEPs), workplace rights, access to healthcare, and support for families. Some advocacy groups also work for increased funding for autism research and services.

Access to Services and Resources: Advocates push for access to early Intervention programs, therapies, support services, and assistive technologies for individuals with autism and their families. Ensuring equitable access to these services is critical in improving the quality of life for individuals on the spectrum.

Employment and Educational Rights: Advocacy efforts in education and employment aim to promote inclusive educational practices and provide employment opportunities for individuals with autism. This includes advocating for special education services, job training programs, workplace accommodations, and equal rights for autistic individuals in the workforce.

Supporting Neurodiversity: Advocacy also focuses on promoting the concept of neurodiversity, which recognizes that neurological differences such as autism are part of natural human variation. Advocates argue that society should embrace and support neurodiverse individuals rather than trying to "cure" or "fix" them. This includes pushing for workplace and educational environments that accommodate a wide range of learning styles and communication methods.

Parent and Family Advocacy: Parents and family members of individuals with autism often engage in advocacy efforts to improve support for their loved ones. Advocacy efforts may include forming local support groups, raising awareness about autism, and pushing for changes in educational and healthcare systems. Many advocacy organizations also provide training and resources for families to navigate the challenges of raising a child or supporting an adult with autism.

Research and advocacy are vital components of advancing our understanding of Autism Spectrum Disorder and ensuring that individuals with autism have the opportunities and support they need to thrive. Through scientific research, we continue to learn more about the causes and effective interventions for autism, while advocacy efforts promote inclusivity, equality, and the acceptance of neurodiverse individuals. By combining the power of research with the passion of advocacy, we can create a world where individuals with autism are empowered, supported, and celebrated for their unique contributions.

CHAPTER 7

Conclusion

Autism Spectrum Disorder (ASD) is a complex and multifaceted condition that affects individuals in diverse ways. As we move forward in our understanding of autism, it is crucial to focus not just on medical and behavioral interventions but also on societal attitudes and inclusivity. The journey toward supporting individuals with autism requires a paradigm shift—one that emphasizes acceptance, respect, and empowerment rather than viewing autism as a problem to be "fixed."

The Evolving Understanding of Autism

Over the years, our understanding of autism has evolved significantly. From early misconceptions that treated autism as a rare disorder to the recognition of it as a spectrum of neurodevelopmental differences, progress has been made in understanding its complexities. Researchers continue to uncover insights into the genetic, neurological, and environmental factors that contribute to autism, which may one day lead to earlier diagnoses and better-targeted interventions. However, it is essential to remember that autism is not a single monolithic condition, but a wide range of experiences, strengths, and challenges.

As we improve our knowledge of autism, it is equally important to focus on what the condition is rather than what it isn't. Rather than attempting to "normalize" individuals with autism or eliminate traits associated with the condition, the future of autism care should focus on creating environments that recognize and support neurodiversity. The concept of neurodiversity champions the idea that autism is part of the natural variation of human experience and that individuals with autism can lead successful and fulfilling lives with the right support.

The Importance of Acceptance and Inclusivity
The path forward for autism involves a societal transformation in how we view and interact with those who have the condition. Promoting acceptance and understanding is key to creating a world where individuals with autism are seen for their unique contributions rather than just their challenges.

Educational Settings: Inclusive educational environments that provide accommodations and individualized support are critical for enabling students with autism to thrive. By embracing diverse learning styles and fostering understanding among peers, schools can help reduce stigma and promote empathy.

Workplaces and Employment: Many individuals with autism have exceptional skills, particularly in fields such as technology, art, and research. Employers who understand the strengths of neurodiverse individuals and offer workplace accommodations can unlock the potential of workers with autism, creating a more inclusive and diverse workforce.

Community Participation: Building communities that are inclusive and accepting of individuals with autism allows them to engage in social, recreational, and cultural activities. This inclusion not only benefits individuals with autism but enriches society as a whole, fostering a deeper understanding of diversity and empathy.

The Need for Comprehensive Support Systems
While acceptance is crucial, it must be paired with tangible support systems that help individuals with autism reach their full potential. These systems include access to early intervention programs, therapy, vocational training, healthcare services, and mental health support. A coordinated effort between families, educators, healthcare professionals, employers, and community organizations is necessary to create a network of care that meets the varied needs of individuals with autism throughout their lives.

Early Intervention: Evidence continues to show that early diagnosis and intervention are crucial for improving outcomes for children with autism. Early interventions that focus on communication, behavior, and social skills can lay the foundation for success in later life.

Lifelong Support: Support should not end with childhood. Adults with autism require continued access to resources such as employment training, mental health services, and independent living assistance to ensure they lead fulfilling, independent lives.

Advocacy and Policy Change: Advocates will play a key role in ensuring that individuals with autism have access to the services, rights, and accommodations they need. Through legislative advocacy and public education campaigns, the rights of individuals with autism must be protected, and opportunities for inclusion and support should be expanded.

Conclusion: A Future of Empowerment and Understanding

The future of autism is one of empowerment, acceptance, and support. As we continue to deepen our understanding of autism and its diverse expressions, we must move beyond the idea of autism as something to be "cured" and instead focus on creating a world where neurodiverse individuals are understood, valued, and supported. By investing in research, advocating for policy changes, fostering inclusive environments, and building comprehensive support systems, we can ensure that individuals with autism not only survive but thrive in society.

The journey forward is not just about addressing the challenges of autism; it is about embracing the richness that neurodiversity brings to our communities, workplaces, and families. Together, we can create a world where individuals with autism are not only accepted for who they are but celebrated for their unique abilities and perspectives.

www.ingramcontent.com/pod-product-compliance
Lightning Source LLC
Chambersburg PA
CBHW051717250726
48653CB00008B/3083